5 MYTHS ABOUT CLASSROOM TECHNOLOGY

How do we integrate digital tools to truly enhance learning?

Matt
RENWICK

ASCD   Alexandria, VA USA

ASCD®

Website: www.ascd.org
E-mail: books@ascd.org

ASCD | arias™

www.ascdarias.org

PAPERBACK ISBN: 978-1-4166-2127-0   ASCD product #SF115069

Also available as an e-book (see Books in Print for the ISBNs).

Library of Congress Cataloging-in-Publication Data

Names: Renwick, Matt.
Title: 5 myths about classroom technology : how do we integrate digital tools to truly enhance learning? / Matt Renwick.
Other titles: Five myths about classroom technology
Description: Alexandria, VA : ASCD, [2015] | Includes bibliographical references.
Identifiers: LCCN 2015038062 | ISBN 9781416621270 (pbk.)
Subjects: LCSH: Educational technology. | Education--Effect of technological innovations on. | Blended learning.
Classification: LCC LB1028.3 .R4535 2015 | DDC 371.33--dc23 LC record available at http://lccn.loc.gov/2015038062

24 23 22 21 20 19 18 17 16 15   1 2 3 4 5 6 7 8 9 10

5 MYTHS ABOUT CLASSROOM TECHNOLOGY

How do we integrate digital tools to truly enhance learning?

Want to earn a free ASCD Arias e-book?
Your opinion counts! Please take 2–3 minutes to give
us your feedback on this publication. All survey
respondents will be entered into a drawing to
win an ASCD Arias e-book.

Please visit
www.ascd.org/ariasfeedback

Thank you!

Technology: Necessary or Nice?

"What would happen if all of the computers in the world suddenly disappeared?" asked Sage French, a blogger and Microsoft intern (French, 2015).

I embedded Sage's screencast with her provocative question on my Kidblog site. Kidblog is a safe and student-friendly blogging platform that allows learners to write and share their thinking with a broader audience. Once my post was finished, I shared it with April Hafermann's 3rd grade classroom in our school, Howe Elementary. Her students were encouraged to respond to this inquiry in the comments section of the post. Here is what they shared:

- If all the computers suddenly disappeared, we wouldn't be able to do school work.
- We couldn't even post anything like this.
- You wouldn't get to do math on the tablets, computers, or phones.
- We wouldn't be able to play fun games on the computers.
- It would be like the 1980s! We would end up using chalkboards.
- It would be boring. Some people might be going crazy!

I always enjoy viewing school and learning through the eyes of our students. I agreed with what they shared. I wanted to add a few thoughts of my own, such as without computers we wouldn't have a school website to connect with families, we wouldn't have online resources for research, we would have only limited ways to show our learning and creative thinking, and we'd have fewer opportunities to develop connections with educators beyond our local colleagues (no social media). Without the connectivity that technology and the Internet provide, it would be a lonely planet indeed.

On the other hand, we often see technology through rose-tinted glasses. To play devil's advocate, what might be some of the benefits of a world without computers? First, no e-mail messages. I can almost hear the collective cheer from school administrators. Beyond small grievances, what might be different if computers were not in our lives? If I am not hunched over a computer screen during the day, that means more time in classrooms, more time with students, and more time to listen to teachers as they share their concerns and celebrations, face-to-face. That doesn't sound so bad.

I believe we struggle with technology in today's schools because *we aren't sure when it is necessary and when it is just nice.* Theories, practices, and applications abound as we try to make sense of what digital tools we should use with both students and staff. Studies to help determine the effectiveness of technology integration are now becoming available but it will be some time before there is consensus on when it is necessary to bring these powerful tools into teaching and learning practices.

So should we wait to integrate? Absolutely not. The opportunities for what is possible when teachers embed technology into instruction are almost endless. If you have ever hosted a Skype chat with an author and your class, observed a student's writing skills improve on his blog, or received a positive note from a mom saying how much she appreciates seeing her child's work in a digital portfolio, you understand the possibilities. The benefits outweigh any risks.

Our focus leads into a big question: How do we integrate digital tools to truly enhance learning? As an elementary school principal and a former teacher, I know this question weighs heavily on educators' minds. We feel external pressure to upgrade instruction, even when we feel what we already do has a positive effect student on learning. However, we are all pushed to do more, so let's explore the attributes of technology and how it can help improve teaching and learning.

As I highlight specific apps, devices, and strategies, I will share real life examples of how they are being used by educators in powerful ways. These educators worked through many hours of professional development, went through many trials and errors, and persevered in using technology to improve student learning. In working through that process alongside my colleagues, I've discovered three main criteria that support smart decisions about using technology in the classroom: access, purpose, and audience. I used those three criteria to create a list of questions and suggestions that are designed to help make smart decisions when considering technology integration within your school or classroom. The list was developed to be applicable to almost any context, but specific enough to provide guidance to implement digital tools thoughtfully and with intent (see the Encore).

The role and potential effect of technology in education is a hot topic. Blogs, websites, professional journals, and social media are filled with many different examples of what works with technology-enhanced instruction. I hope you find this guide to debunking myths about technology in education to be a helpful next step in making decisions that will have a powerful influence on how our students learn.

Myth #1: Technology is easy to learn and use.

Among my many duties is to serve as a guest teacher when we cannot find a substitute teacher. During a recent stint in a 1st grade classroom, I took over teacher Lisa Black's literacy block. Here is what was involved—including using technology —on my end:

- Read the lesson plans.
- Reread the lesson plans.
- Turn on the projector and document camera.
- Check the literacy stations to make sure they are prepared.
- Review the learning expectations with the students.
- Disperse students to assigned stations.
- Monitor student activity, redirecting as needed.

- Troubleshoot a CD player that isn't playing an audiobook in the listening center.
- Send a student to the office to get new batteries for the CD player.
- Confer with a student about a book to assess his reading comprehension.
- Tweet a picture of a student as she finishes creating a story she wrote on a memorable event in her life.
- Help the returning student install the batteries in the CD player.
- Confer with another student on his writing.
- Download a reading app to the four classroom iPads.
- Check on the student who has been in the bathroom a little too long.
- Ring the chimes to call the students to the front for a public conference.
- Wake up the projector (it was muted to save energy and hide the screen).
- Facilitate a public conference with the student writer and use the document camera to project her writing on the screen for the whole class to see.
- Ask a student to rotate students' names on the board assigning literacy stations.
- Direct students to their new assignments.

I am sure Lisa would attest to the accuracy of this description of a slice of a day in the life of a 1st grade teacher. It is experiences like this that help me stay grounded when we want to introduce new technology to students and teachers.

As a principal for close to a decade, these experiences are valuable reminders about what it's like to be "it" in the classroom. Administrators can become forgetful about the complexities of teaching.

We all forget about the challenges associated with what we do every day. I am reminded of that when I observe consultants and experts at conferences. In this case, I'm thinking about how they sometimes fail to communicate the difficulty of integrating technology into instruction. It's not as simple as providing a computer for every student. A thousand things can go wrong. The tablets didn't charge, a screen freezes, the wireless connection is spotty. Unfortunately, the fix is usually not as simple as switching out the batteries.

Technology is not necessarily easy to learn or use. Asking teachers to implement digital tools can be daunting even when they are given the rationale for using the technology, proper training, time to practice, and accessible support. But with these elements in place, bringing technology into classrooms and schools can be a worthwhile effort regardless of the learning curve.

Rationale for the Technology

Without providing substantial reasons for adding technology to a teacher's life, we significantly lessen the chance that it will be embedded into instruction as an essential part of student learning. We can cite the research supporting technology and provide myriad examples of it in action. Yet, a clear rationale for introducing technology into the classroom is an essential step. I learned this lesson the hard way. When we first introduced digital portfolios into classrooms, my agenda resembled a grocery list of topics to cover (Renwick, 2014). My initial thinking was the more, the better.

After some candid conversations among faculty members, however, we realized that if a technology tool was to be implemented with fidelity in the classroom, we needed time to discuss it. Developing a rationale for a significant change provides benefits for learning organizations. First, it helps create a common language for the attributes for technology-enhanced instruction. For example, we understand **access** refers not only to the number of devices available, but also to the level of filtering of web content, the strength of the wireless signal in classrooms, and the appropriateness of the mobile device and software for the learners. Second, a rationale can provide structure when preparing instruction. For example, when a teacher is developing a unit of study, she can focus on the **purpose** to determine the "what" of learning. Then she can identify the "how" (**access**) and the "who" (**audience**). These constraints can create helpful limitations when designing learning activities for all students.

A third benefit of developing a shared rationale when discussing digital integration is how it filters out less effective methods of instruction before they take root in classrooms. When a technology tool or strategy is applied to a set of criteria and it doesn't meet the mark, there is a better chance that it will not be used.

See Figure 1 for an example of the rationale behind our technology decisions.

FIGURE 1: Consider Access, Purpose, and Audience to Determine When Technology is Necessary or Nice

1. Access

• It is **nice** to purchase one type of device for every learner, provide initial training, and allow staff and students to explore what's possible.

• It is **necessary** to assess infrastructure, school needs, and student needs as well as purchase specific tools and schedule ongoing training.

2. Purpose

• It is **nice** to use trial-and-error with the technology and select a curriculum unit or lesson plan that allows for its use.

• It is **necessary** to design curriculum focused on essential knowledge and skills and apply technology within the learning progression.

3. Audience

• It is **nice** to house student work on the devices or in the cloud for easy retrieval.

• It is **necessary** to publish student work for those outside the classroom to view and give feedback and affirmation.

Notice how uses of technology that may have a small influence on student learning are listed under "nice." Using technology as a replacement activity, say a digital game on math facts instead of a worksheet, is not inherently a bad thing. In fact, it might be a slight upgrade to the worksheet if it keeps students engaged longer in the learning and the game provides feedback. Additionally, initial forays into technology-enhanced instruction may be at a basic level of learning (it was in our school). If you separate the nice from the necessary activities, you'll have both a vision of what's possible and a progression toward essential uses of technology in schools.

Proper Training and Time to Practice

Proper training for any new initiative involves a well-prepared meeting agenda that anticipates teachers' needs and questions. Send the agenda to participants at least a day in advance to allow them a chance to see what will be covered, download any necessary applications, and develop questions. Another benefit of sending the agenda early is that teachers sometimes find answers to their questions or solve problems before the meeting begins—often by seeking out a colleague.

Our school's professional development activities usually happen after school and we try to schedule these events as far in advance as possible. As a father of two young children, I understand this need. Once the training starts, the time is roughly split in thirds. We use one-third for modeling how to use the technology and two-thirds for trying out the technology and asking/answering questions. I used to have a long list of agenda items that I planned to cover. Now I try to focus on a few essential skills and to help the staff become confident in using the technology. If I do write a lengthy agenda, I highlight a few essential topics that we will cover. If we get to more than anticipated, that's gravy.

When presenting hardware or software to the entire school, I sometimes defer to another staff member. As a principal, I no longer "speak teacher" well enough to answer questions about logistics and challenges. My role as the school leader in professional development settings has transitioned from lead teacher to facilitator, colleague, and learner. When trying to integrate technology, know that the best trainers are often within your own school.

Once we develop a collective level of proficiency in using a tool or strategy, it is beneficial to provide staff with a choice. As an example, our most recent technology training provided teachers a choice of learning how to use tools such as Google Apps for Education or Evernote for curating professional learning artifacts. We developed the agenda using feedback from a staff survey about our previous professional development experience. Two staff members led the Google session while I guided the Evernote group. Voice and choice in what our colleagues want to learn enhances excellent training and time to practice using these digital tools.

Example of Practice: Innovation Nights

We have monthly sessions for all school members. We host the session on a different weekday each month so that people who have conflicts on specific days can attend. One faculty member and I facilitate the training. We start by reteaching the basics of how to use the main device (the iPad), such as how to take a screenshot (home button + power button). The review helps to build fluency and then we go into a specific tool, using the gradual release of responsibility for teaching how to use the tablets (Frey, Fisher, & Gonzalez, 2013).

In our case, we have adopted the FreshGrade app to curate student learning within digital portfolios. Faculty are provided a review of the basics of this application, such as adding lessons and selecting the type of assessment used for that lesson.

Then, teachers provide demonstrations and guidance for their students in how to upload their learning artifacts and add reflections. Parents and guardians are involved as well. Newsletters and messages are sent to encourage families to check out their child's portfolio, leave a comment, and discuss the learning activity at home.

These evenings used to be called Technology Nights. Upon reflection, there was a problem with this practice. Our focus was on technology. This created a separation between the technology topics that we were teaching and how they were to be used or how they worked in the classroom. We adopted the concept of "innovation," defined as "putting new ideas into practice" (Robinson & Aronica, 2015). Using the theme of Innovation Nights allows us to address skills and applications of talents in a variety of areas. For example, school staff and members of the community could present on topics including computer coding, grant writing for classroom resources, and using social media for personal learning.

Accessible Support

Have you noticed that when you open up the box of a new digital device, there is no operator's manual? Welcome to learning in today's world. The expectations for using computers, tablets, and other technologies has evolved from 20 sequential steps for getting started to simply "Press start." In part that's because devices are now easier to use.

Another reason for the lack of instruction and support out of the box is the wealth of information available online. One of my mantras when conducting any sort of training is "If you don't know the answer, search YouTube." YouTube is a video-sharing site to which someone somewhere in the world has most likely posted a screencast with the answer, such as how to embed a video into a post on Kidblog. (Yes, I checked before posting Sage French's video for our 3rd graders.)

Personal Learning Networks (PLNs) are also great sources of information for educators. PLNs are defined by Will Richardson and Rob Mancabelli as "a set of connections to people and resources both online and offline who enrich our learning" (2011, p. 21). Our school provided explicit training in how to develop and maintain these types of connections with other educators and classrooms. Social media tools, such as Twitter, Blogger, and Facebook, are frequently used to share student learning with families and the larger community. Many teachers collect teaching ideas on Pinterest, a visual bookmarking tool, and some go beyond that to share information within online educational forums.

The way we support technology integration in schools has expanded. Our needs may go beyond what was traditionally provided. Support personnel now do more than figure out what is wrong with the wireless or why a computer screen froze. School leaders need to commit to addressing the needs of teachers and students while stretching to see how we can augment learning experiences with technology. Although it can be difficult and take a great deal of time to learn how to incorporate technology into our classrooms and schools, the payoffs for using technology in *necessary* ways are worth the resources.

Reflection

- How do you make decisions in your school about technology?
- Think about a recent decision in your school or district regarding technology. Did you consider purpose, audience, and access when making that decision? How might considering these three elements change the way decisions are made in your school?

Myth #2: Technology is expensive.

Our school started implementing mobile devices in classrooms in 2011. As a pilot, we asked teachers to use one tablet in their classrooms for a semester and to report on their experiences. Out of 35 professional educators, 12 expressed interest. The lack of interest may surprise you, but the staff expressed many reservations. What if I drop it? Are the students allowed to hold it? Can I use it for personal reasons? We addressed these questions as we learned together, meeting after school to share our ups and downs and to create strategies for next steps in our technology plan.

The money for purchasing the tablets came from our Title I budget (more than 60 percent of our families live in poverty). Yes, we could have used the funds for more books for our students, more staff, or more professional development. Instead,

I considered these initial forays into mobile learning as a private company might view investing money and energies into research and development. Schools have to be at the edge of what's possible—we are an institution for learning. Concepts such as digital citizenship and content curation should also be part of the curriculum.

From that standpoint, stating that technology is expensive is a misnomer. Yes, the money needed for infrastructure, such as a strong wireless system and a reasonable ratio of devices to students, can be considerable. The opportunity for our students and staff to learn to use technology and access online resources outweigh the initial costs. And we considered what technology use might remove from our budgets. For instance, the option of cutting spending on traditional textbooks can be a trade-off for the access and use of state-of-the-art technology.

Time and Money

Richardson and Mancabelli point out the potential savings in both dollars spent and efficiencies discovered by using technology in *Personal Learning Networks: Using the Power of Connections to Transform Education*. For example, their prediction that "by 2015, a computer that students could use effectively for both classroom and personal use will cost about $200" (2011, p. 120) has proven accurate. Chromebooks, mostly web devices that use Google's operating system, are in this price range. They have a full keyboard and a folding screen and are used wirelessly to access Google's free suite of online software. With this hardware, the learner can access Google

Apps for Education to work collaboratively on writing in the Google Docs application and on multimedia presentations in Google Slides. Drafts and final products are saved online within Google Drive cloud storage. For the cost of a textbook or two, these devices also allow access to other web-based applications. In justifying the cost of the technology, you may want to consider the paper, writing utensils, and folders that your school may not have to purchase.

If your school does not qualify for extra funding, there are creative ways to make your goals for technology-enhanced instruction a reality. For example, Donors Choose (www.donorschoose.org) is a highly respected website that encourages teachers to post project ideas that need funding. Oprah Winfrey and Stephen Colbert have supported many teacher requests. One of our teachers, Michelle Steffes, received a donation from Donors Choose to purchase a classroom subscription to *Scholastic Storyworks*, a monthly magazine that is rich with content and addresses the many areas of language arts, including digital literacy. In addition, our tablet initiative was started with a $1,000 grant from a local community foundation, Incourage (incouragecf.org). The two iPad tablets we purchased and tried out with students gave us opportunities to explore how to teach and learn with just a few devices.

School funds are not the only factor when preparing to go more mobile and more connected with learning. Time is another factor. Connected learning can reduce the time that it takes to set up, monitor, and assess student projects. In our 5th grade classrooms, teachers taught students how to use Google Sites for their digital portfolios. This tool is a website creator that can be developed from the ground up by anyone. Students were taught how to save and organize their work in Google Drive, upload it to their personal site and then add reflections to their learning artifacts. Teachers can focus less on organizing and tracking papers and folders, and instead plan periodic pauses in instruction for students to reflect in digital spaces. Learners can look back on their work and highlight where they met standards of excellence in their portfolios. The teacher's role becomes more of a coach in providing feedback and helping students reflect. The lion's share of these efforts rest on the students' shoulders.

Example of Practice: The One Device Classroom

If you work in a school where funds are always hard to find, don't fret. Some of the smartest ideas for connecting students to the world come from classrooms where technology is limited. In fact, most of our primary classrooms have only four or five mobile devices. These limitations spurred creativity in how teachers leverage technology to improve student learning.

In Bri Crubel's 3rd grade classroom, images of students at work along with captions are regularly posted on the classroom's Twitter account using only one iPad. Bri uses that technology to tweet (post on Twitter) regularly about their learning lives. One day, Bri posted a picture of students participating in a social studies simulation with the caption, "Open for business." In the image, two girls were exchanging money for goods. In another post, the students' feet are in a circle on the floor, celebrating Crazy Sock Day. Families love to see fun pictures and we enjoy the benefit of celebrating our school's rich diversity using a digital platform.

Although there is nothing profound in any specific tweet, it is the fact of sharing their daily learning and experiences that can be powerful. First, Bri embedded the Twitter timeline on her webpage so that anyone connected to the classroom (e.g., parents and guardians) can observe the students' learning without having to create and log into an account. Second, the act of tweeting involves modeling and applying several literacy skills expected of students, such as proper grammar, clear ideas, and summarization. The 140-character limit of Twitter requires users to be creative in describing the image that is being published. Third, Bri now has a repository of artifacts to use in her own professional evaluation process. She can come back to these posts to use them as evidence of student understanding and for reflection on her practice. Finally, Bri's students used Twitter to connect with other students in classrooms beyond our school walls for collaborative projects.

What if you don't have access to a mobile device but want to document student learning online? Consider a digital camera with wireless capabilities. Sherry Marzofka, a kindergarten teacher, purchased a camera that allows her to post images directly to her classroom's Facebook page. Once given permission by parents or guardians to share student images within this private page, Sherry can grant access to her students' family members. One event that she documented involved students creating buildings out of graham crackers, chocolate frosting, and marshmallows. The goal: The structure must be able to stand freely in the face of a driving wind (a house fan).

As students created their structures, Sherry took pictures to document their progress. Sharing images from the classroom has proven to be a discussion starter among families and students. The refrigerator door has received an update with the possibilities from social media.

As you can see, access to only one piece of technology has not hampered the sharing of student learning that occurs in Bri's and Sherry's classrooms. If you asked the students' parents, they would likely agree that digitally documenting these learning experiences are necessary in today's connected world.

Faulty Logic

Education tends to perpetuate the idea that more is better. We need more money, more staffing, more room, and more time. Often this is true. The push for more technology in schools doesn't always follow the same logic. We often place a priority on the globally connected experience over the local and likely more meaningful connections we can have inside our classrooms.

Sometimes one piece of technology is unnecessary, and possibly not even nice, but rather a hindrance to a lesson. In Gabi Scheunemann's 1st grade classroom, she set up a whole class discussion around the essential question, "What is and is not technology?" She would display and name an item, such as a pencil, and then have the students split into groups to discuss as teams. Once student teams shared their collective thinking, Gabi guided her group to clear up misconceptions and move closer to a deeper understanding of technology in their lives. One revelation was that not all technology required electricity.

For young people who have grown up in a digital world, these are necessary conversations. Adding technology to the lesson would have been a distraction. We'll explore this idea more in the next section, when we question the rationale of having technology in the hands of every student.

Technology doesn't have to be digital or expensive. We can do a lot with what we already have and be savvy about finding funding for the technology we need. These constraints can also help us be smarter about when technology is necessary and when it is nice, keeping the focus on opportunities for meaningful student learning.

Reflection

- If you could pick only one type of technology for your classroom or context, what would it be? What would make it a necessary part of your practice?
- How might having access to only one mobile device in a classroom still lead to better instruction and student learning?

Myth #3: Technology should be in the hands of every student.

I get e-mail messages from companies and consultants proclaiming that they have the answer for the one device to every student (1:1) solution for my school. Why is it assumed that schools have a problem in the first place and that a device in every student's hands would be a solution? When every student has access, notes some technology providers, then and only then can our learners tap into the world of knowledge.

Many highly respected educators also jumped on the one-device-per-learner bandwagon. For example, I agree with much of what Richardson and Mancabelli have to say regarding technology in schools, but they also assert that each student should have his own device once past primary school (2011, p. 116). This is where they and I diverge philosophically. I lean more toward first assessing why 1:1 is necessary and not just nice, and then look to provide access that will meet every student's needs.

It's All About Context

Proclaiming that all schools need to go 1:1 is akin to suggesting that all students benefit from homework. Yes, there is some evidence that shows homework can increase learning for some students, but it largely is dependent on the age of the student and how homework is used. For example, older students are more likely to benefit from extra studying outside school than younger students (Hattie, 2009). Taking that same approach, considering child development and purpose for the hardware is a better way to implement technology into classrooms.

I use the term "technology" generally. Digital tools don't have to be mobile. Although digital tools are increasingly portable, the shelf life for tablets and laptops is shorter than desktops. When considering which device to use, you'll need to consider your options. In addition, it is easier to supervise students when the screens are all facing one way in the classroom. Students tucked in a corner with their tablets may lead to more off-task behavior, such as looking up funny cat videos (which is tempting for anyone, me included).

Also, I hear teachers who worry that going 1:1 with tablets or laptops increases screen time for their students. Any time schools invest dollars into resources, educators feel an obligation to get the most out of the investment. More is better, right? Sound reasoning, except that this is not always the case with technology. For instance, most medical professionals recommend limiting screen time and creating "tech-free" zones for young people (American Academy of Pediatrics, 2015). How many districts consider this before handing a device to their students? And, if the students are to take the technology home, that brings up loss, damage, and other issues that schools have to tackle.

Consider this student-to-device ratio recommendation, a blend of the research by Sugata Mitra (2010) and my own experiences and observations in schools.

Grade	Recommended Student-to-Device Ratio
K–2	3:1
3–5	2:1
6–8	1:1 access, such as a laptop or tablet cart
9–12	1:1 environment, such as Bring Your Own Device (BYOD)

Context is everything. One device for every student may be necessary when each student is working to develop a final draft of an essay or report on the same deadline. Other times, one device for a collaborative group can lead to deep conversations among students, which may have been skipped if each learner had a laptop. So is going to one device per student a bad thing? In some contexts, no. In fact, it is often necessary. Consider the following scenarios where 1:1 access is essential to ensure every student has an opportunity for an appropriate education.

Students with Special Needs. Providing access to certain technologies for some of our most at-risk learners is an absolute necessity. Specific apps and devices can help students with special needs perform tasks that they couldn't do otherwise.

For some students, reading and writing is difficult. Students in our district have challenges involving dyslexia, fine motor processing, and language delays. Technology can help. One of the best tools that almost all devices include is voice recognition software, whether Google Voice, Apple's Siri, or Dragon Dictation. Software like these allow students to press a microphone button, speak, and the words are transcribed onto the screen. For students who struggle to put ideas on paper, a speech-to-text application can help them bypass that part of the writing process and convey what they want to say and then revise it.

Teachers can take this idea a step further with word-predictive technology. Certain apps, including Spell Better, will predict the next word a student is trying to type or say. The student can accept the suggestion or ask the software to offer another word within the context of the sentence. It is surprisingly accurate. In Sue Morzewski's special education class, I observed a 5th grade student write a book summary using this application. Once she was done, the app read her writing aloud so that she could revise her work until she was ready to publish it. Without this application, it is unlikely she would have stayed engaged so long or written so carefully.

English-Language Learners. For English-language learners, their school experience is often learning-by-immersion. Many students are fortunate if they have more than one person working with them who speaks their native language. One of the best tools to serve this population are read-to-me digital books. Many of these apps, including iBooks, offer a variety of titles that include *audio* along with the text and illustrations. The books are often read aloud by a professional narrator and the choices in authentic texts are growing. One of my favorite publishers is Oceanhouse Media. They provide high-quality production and high-interest texts, including titles from Dr. Seuss and nonfiction from the Smithsonian Institution. With many of these digitally enhanced books, the reader can highlight specific vocabulary to get a dynamic definition. An animation or other visual representation pops up to convey the meaning of the word, a technique which has shown to better support vocabulary acquisition when compared to print (Korat, Levin, Ben-Shabt, Shneor, & Bokovza, 2014).

Many apps allow for literacy creation instead of just consumption. One of the best is Book Creator. Students create their own digital books, complete with images, drawing, text, and audio narration. Once ready, the final product can be published in a variety of ways. Students can save their books and add them to a classroom listening library or upload them to YouTube for friends and family to view. In addition, books can be printed out as a PDF, though they obviously lose the audio component. Students can become published authors by exporting their books as an epub file, ready to be uploaded into the iBooks store. From there, anyone in the world can download it onto their e-readers. Apps like Book Creator support the notion that people learn best by doing.

Rural, Urban, and Virtual School Settings. In areas where access to the Internet is not widely or easily available, providing connectivity is a priority. For example, a science teacher who serves as the whole science department in a small school community experiences inherent limitations related to resources and how many classes she can offer. With access to the Internet, however, that teacher and her students can find a plethora of online, blended, and post-secondary offerings that are specific to students' interests and needs. In rural and urban areas where it is difficult to hire a highly qualified teacher, especially in the areas of mathematics and sciences, giving students access to classes and essential content is a critical component of their education. Online learning may be the best option in these situations.

Virtual schools also provide a specific service for learners who, for a variety of reasons, cannot attend regular public education. Several providers offer online curriculum software that students can access, either from home or through a local school district. In my own district, Wisconsin Rapids Public Schools, students can apply to enroll in our virtual school.

Once accepted, they select the online curriculum most conducive to their needs and the school supplies a laptop. We have found many students who are homeschooled like this option. They complete their core curriculum work at home and then come into the public school's brick-and-mortar setting for encore classes such as music and art.

Students with physical or mental health challenges can also benefit from having an online curriculum and a laptop or tablet at their disposal. The arrangement can be temporary, such as when a student has an acute injury that prevents him from physically coming to school. The timeline for this arrangement is dependent on the student's specific circumstances. In some districts where online coursework is not available, schools have allowed students to use video chats or voice calls to engage in learning. Students with severe social anxiety that prevents them from attending a physical classroom might also benefit from a virtual learning environment.

Independent Learning Projects for Gifted Students. Students on both ends of the achievement spectrum often need more support in school. Daniel, a 2nd grader in Janice Heyroth's class, is a high-achieving math student. A few minutes after his teacher briefly explains the concept of the day, Daniel shows mastery of the essential understandings through a quick check. He spends the rest of math class involved in getting on a skill-focused math app on one of the classroom iPads. Unfortunately, this holds his attention for only a short time. Gifted learners have a tendency to become bored quickly if the content they are learning is easy or redundant.

Both Daniel's parents and Janice realized that he needed something different. More of the same was not equating with more learning, and technology alone failed to keep his attention. Also, always being away from the classroom community while working with the math app could have had an isolating effect. After inquiring about Daniel's interests and discovering that he enjoyed biology, the teacher and I set up a weather and bird-watching station in the library. The students from Daniel's class filled two bird feeders with different types of seeds and hung them on a free-standing pole. A digital weather sensor was placed next to the window.

To provide the audience that will increase the purpose for his work, Daniel is given full access to an iPad and his Kidblog page. He could upload pictures of the bird feeders, the current weather for the day, and then add comments about what he observed at his class's science station. Text, images, video, and links are published for others to read and comment on online. His teacher turned off the permission feature of Daniel's blog page, giving him more responsibility to post the day's content for his classmates and parents.

Daniel's blog led to conversations about what species of birds live in our area, as well as how the weather might affect their activity. The direct application of important mathematical concepts, such as understanding decimals and place value, was important work for Daniel. What he documented and shared affected what he and his peers learned and brought him closer with his classroom community, instead alienating him. Most important, Daniel's role changed from a math student to a scientist and reporter. And like these professionals, Daniel used the technology only when it was needed and with intent.

Finding the Right Ratio

Getting technology into the hands of students does not have to be a rush job. Before considering any kind of technology initiative, first look at the research that supports it. For example, Sugata Mitra, a social scientist who started School in the Cloud (www.schoolinthecloud.org), found from his research that an optimal ratio of students to device is 4:1. When students have to share a computer as they consume and create online content, they have to collaborate about what they are learning and come to consensus regarding what they will produce and share. As noted previously, our school has a somewhat similar ratio of devices per student. Start with your students' needs and consider the learning context before deciding on the ratio.

So should secondary schools reconsider 1:1 computing initiatives? You'll hear that "Students at the secondary level can handle these digital responsibilities with a purpose." And, "They need access to essential content only found online." But when we add one more digital connection to the lives of teenagers, what gets pushed out? Are our efforts to be more connected truly necessary, or just another nice and possibly counterproductive offering? It is in the last two sections that we explore this issue and others related to the effect of technology on student learning and always being "on."

Reflection

- How has your school determined the amount of access students are provided for learning? Has the process been based on needs (necessary) or wants (nice)?
- Situation: A sales representative for a technology provider shows up at your door, selling the virtues of a 1:1 school environment. What questions might you ask before making a decision?

Myth #4: Technology improves student learning.

Kentaro Toyama, a professor at the University of Michigan, states that adding technology to schools won't necessarily improve student learning. After a decade of professional research and personal study, he found that when digital devices are brought into the learning mix, the outcome is largely dependent on what was already being taught and how. "Technology's primary effect is to amplify human forces, so in education, technologies amplify whatever pedagogical capacity is already there" (Toyama, 2015).

Toyama's research results should give educators pause as they consider implementing technology initiatives in their classrooms, schools, and districts. How does a school or district know that they have the instructional pieces in place that would allow for a successful technology integration process? Will this process include lots of time, training, and necessary tools to ensure success? The belief that teachers cannot be great without integrating technology into their instruction bypasses the fact that no amount of technology will improve poor teaching.

The Reality of Technology's Effect on Student Learning

The actions of schools and teachers in classrooms has been a focus of John Hattie's work. In his seminal resource *Visible Learning: A Synthesis of Over 800 Meta-Analyses Relating to Achievement* (2009), he found that computer-assisted instruction was not correlated with a year's worth of growth for a year's input. In fact, Hattie contends, there is little indication that the future will hold anything different regarding the effect of technology-enhanced instruction and student learning. "There is no correlation . . . that the effect from computers is increasing with the sophistication of the technology" (p. 221). In other words, we shouldn't be holding our breath for that great app or tool to make a large difference in learning outcomes for students.

What the work of these researchers tells us is that *it is not what we use regarding technology in schools, but how we use it.* The research reminds us of the importance of developing a powerful and clear purpose for learning and then determining how technology might enhance or even transform these experiences. Our improvements to instruction can be nice and even necessary with just a little bit of thought.

How we use digital tools within our instruction can have a positive effect on student understanding. For example, Hattie offers six situations in which using computers (e.g., desktops, tablets) in classrooms can enhance already effective instruction:

1. When there is a diversity of teaching strategies.

2. When there is teacher training in the use of computers as a teaching and learning tool.

3. When there are multiple opportunities for learning (e.g., deliberative practice, increasing time on task).

4. When the student, not the teacher, is in "control" of learning.

5. When peer learning is optimized.

6. When feedback is optimized. (Hattie, 2009, p. 221–227)

Let's look at how this might apply to the classroom and then assess the level of effectiveness using Hattie's guidelines.

Blended Learning

Blended learning can be defined as "a spectrum of teaching modes that combine traditional modes of face-to-face instruction with work done online" (Tucker, 2012, p. 24).

Due to declining enrollment at our school, we used blended learning within a multigrade environment to keep class sizes equitable. One class included 4th and 5th graders. A challenge with this set up is trying to teach two curriculums in one year, especially in a standards-driven environment. Lisa Sonnenberg volunteered for the assignment. A dozen laptops were purchased to help differentiate instruction, giving her classroom a 2:1 ratio. Before school started, Lisa participated in a summer district course that focused on how to use a learning management system, or LMS. An LMS is a digital platform that can hold a variety of content and media for online, personalized instruction. It can also facilitate peer-to-peer conversations, as well as collect student learning artifacts for later assessment.

The LMS that Lisa learned how to use is called Moodle (https://moodle.org/). It is a free, online learning platform that allows the teacher to create units of study using video, images, and online-based content. Moodle gave Lisa the ability to embed links to relevant articles and media and include clear directions for her students within the platform. When it was time for 4th graders to study Wisconsin landforms, they opened their laptops and got started. Students could proceed at their own pace. The personalization of instruction gave students who processed information more slowly the necessary time to develop a deeper understanding. To assess learning during the online courses, Lisa added a digital tool called PoodLL. This plugin allowed students to share their answers to questions through drawings or audio recordings instead of having to use multiple choice or short answer responses. Students with dyslexia and related disabilities found this function user-friendly because it broke through literacy barriers and allowed them to show what they learned and what they are able to do with that learning.

Lisa also used eduCanon, an online learning environment for video lessons, to assess student learning within a Moodle. This plugin allows the teacher to create stopping points within a video and pose a question for the learner. The results from this quick check of understanding are sent to Lisa in a report that she can view later. There are no papers to take home or homework to dig for in desks. More important, the students seemed to enjoy this change in learning and that they could respond to instruction in multiple ways.

Developing a LMS using Moodles helped Lisa find more time to provide face-to-face instruction for the 5th grade social studies curriculum. Once the 5th grade lesson was done, she transitioned to the 4th graders to check on their work. Lisa listened to their audio responses, added comments, and then conferred with students to provide feedback in person. She spent more time guiding students who needed her support toward essential understandings while allowing others to move to the next module. In addition, by moving the opportunity for direct instruction to the individual students (instead of a lecture for the whole class) often called "flipped learning" (Flipped Learning Network, 2014), Lisa had more opportunities for meaningful student discussions and learning simulations, such as hosting a mock legislation process. Flipped learning, a form of blended learning, helped her become a more efficient and responsive teacher.

In reflecting after the first year of having a blended learning, multigrade classroom, we came to some conclusions. First, the work involved in teaching with a learning management system isn't reduced. The work just shifted, from mostly during and after instruction to before and during instruction. Second, some students initially struggled with this format. They wanted to be told what to know, instead of finding out for themselves. This is probably a result of what our students are used to in schools, especially those who have learned how to play the game. Third, there should eventually be a gradual shift in instructional design, from the teacher exclusively developing the coursework, to the students and teacher cocreating pathways toward essential understandings.

Assessing Instructional Practice

The definition of best practice is "serious, thoughtful, informed, responsible, state-of-the-art teaching." Hattie's suggested situations previously listed would seem to serve as criteria for this definition. Let's do a crosscheck between the criteria and Lisa's use of blended learning:

- *Was there a diversity of teaching practices?* Most definitely. Lisa tapped into multiple media formats, provided different pathways for delivering the content, and allowed for several options for students to respond to the posted inquiries.
- *Was teacher training provided in the use of computers as a teaching and learning tool?* Yes, in the form of summer training. It should be noted that the professional development Lisa participated in was not a smorgasbord of apps to try out in the classroom. Rather, it was a deep focus on using one tool (Moodle) to address specific student and curriculum needs.
- *Were there multiple opportunities for learning?* It should be no surprise that students were very attentive when exploring a lesson through the LMS on Moodle, probably more so than during a traditional lecture on the humanities. The integration of video, images, and primary artifacts, along with thoughtful

questions embedded within the content, kept the students engaged.

- *Were students in control of their own learning?* Somewhat, in the sense that responses to the questions within the modules allowed students to respond in multiple ways. Also, students could work at their own pace through the modules. Teaching students to create a unit of study for their peers using Moodle would truly transfer ownership of the learning.
- *Was peer learning optimized?* Students could comment on the work of their classmates to acknowledge accurate thinking or to provide guidance if a mistake was found. Within these walls, both digitally and physically, there was a sense of community, where everyone cared about each other's learning journey toward success.
- *Was feedback optimized?* One of her students, Sarah, showed me how she can go back in and check for feedback from the teacher. She was visibly excited to see how she did on the assessment, with a level of interest I don't regularly see with a standard paper and pencil test.

Given this assessment, it appears that Lisa's use of technology is beyond nice—and is very necessary. The use of blended learning was essential because of her multigrade classroom and the need to address two curriculums. Maybe more important, blended learning is essential because *it changed how Lisa taught.* She no longer had to follow the traditional method of instruction, with too much time spent talking and not enough on teaching. She could more readily meet students where they were, by allowing them to move at their own pace and providing guidance only when needed. This approach to developing independent learners is something we need to consider beyond specific situations such as Lisa's. In the next section, we look at a secondary level example of how blended learning can be applied to encourage independence.

The use of technology in and of itself does not significantly improve learning. A student filling out a mindless worksheet on a mobile device is not learning any more than if he were filling out a mindless worksheet on a piece of paper. But when we use technology thoughtfully and consider the *how* as much as the *what*, we have the potential to improve both teaching and learning.

Reflection

- The mixed age classroom prompted a need not for the technology itself, but for a change in teaching with the help of technology. Can you think of a situation in your context where constraints have required technology to enhance the way student learn?
- What might be the pros and cons of allowing students to develop a lesson or unit of study using Moodle for their peers? Do the pros outweigh the cons? Why or why not?

Myth #5: Technology is a distraction.

This myth is worthy of a closer investigation. Here is a personal example: During the writing of this text, I lost my smartphone. At first, I found it hard to adjust to the loss. I kept reaching for it to check social media feeds, e-mail messages, and texts. Not having my "mini-computer" made me feel like I had lost a part of me.

After a day or so, I started to adapt. If I left school, I made sure my office staff knew where I would be and gave them a phone number in case of an emergency. I couldn't check e-mail messages regularly, yet I didn't fall behind in my correspondence. When I visited a classroom, I felt more attentive during the learning activities. There was no gadget to distract myself with when I found my attention waning.

After almost a week, our school social worker found my smartphone in our staff resource room. I was a bit hesitant to take it back. Although I missed the ability to snap pictures of classroom activities to share on our school Twitter account, I found myself more fully present during the activities. Not having my phone also reminded me how different the process of writing by hand can be—I enjoyed writing the first draft of this very passage in a paper notebook. And, I discovered that I am less susceptible to the temptations of social media when it is not readily available. Also, before my phone and I were reunited, I spent the better part of a day handwriting notes of gratitude for my staff members. The personal nature of this type of communication lends itself much better to the printed word than a text or e-mail message.

Distractions, or Distractible?

In his book *Hamlet's BlackBerry: Building a Good Life in the Digital Age,* William Powers explores how we have always struggled with and handled distractions. He had his own disconnected experience, accidentally dropping his smartphone in the water while trying to launch his boat off of Cape Cod. Once Powers assessed the situation, he noticed that his involuntary isolation was not all bad. "Just minutes ago, I was embarrassed and angry at myself for drowning my phone. Now that it's gone and connecting is no longer an option, I like what's happening" (2010, p. 40).

What Powers is referring to, this feeling of disconnectedness, is the creation of a healthy gap between the connected world and oneself. It is a state of distance from everything that life offers, which we rarely accept. "What if someone needs to reach me while I am away?" is a typical reason we tether ourselves to the world by always bringing a smartphone wherever we go. But in how many situations is it an absolute necessity to be reachable? I bet if you thought back on your previous trips, both near and far, you'd find that being connected was more of a convenience than a necessity.

So what's the harm in always being connected? Sharing what is happening in school and conversing with educators in online communities can improve the learning experience.

Powers suggests that it is not being connected that causes the problems, but that if we are *always* connected, we never have time to reflect on our learning and be alone with our thoughts. "New technologies form new crowds. And the better they are at it, the more eagerly they are adopted. However, because they tend to increase the individual's exposure to the crowd and ramp up the busyness, they strain the mind and the spirit. Thus, it becomes essential to find escape hatches" (Powers, 2010, p. 122). It is in our time away from the ever-flowing stream of information where learning at a deeper level is more likely to occur.

Rethinking Engagement

Mobile devices, with their applications and notifications, are designed to capture our attention. As an assistant principal for four years, I had one drawer in my desk devoted entirely to holding confiscated students' cell phones. Banning cell phones from classrooms to keep students' attention is like blaming the pan for a poorly cooked meal. Maybe the problem is in the ingredients—whether those in the lesson or the pan. To eat or not to eat; to pay attention or not to pay attention. Technology in classrooms doesn't have to be an either/or proposition, but rather an intentional decision based on the lesson for that day.

Technology itself does not distract or engage learners. Technology, whether hardware or software, is a conduit that allows learners to develop understandings and create unique ways of conveying knowledge and skills. Sometimes, instead of needing to escape from technology, it's the technology itself that provides a healthy escape. Danah Boyd, principal researcher at Microsoft Research, notes that the desire to escape is especially strong with adolescents. "We've locked them indoors because we see the physical world as more dangerous than ever before, even though by almost every measure, we live in the safest society to date. We put unprecedented demands on our kids, maxing them out with structured activities, homework and heavy expectations" (Boyd, 2015). In our attempts to keep kids safe, families may actually be encouraging their children to become more connected with friends online, states Boyd. "They aren't addicted to the computer; they're addicted to interaction, and being around their friends. Children, and especially teenagers, don't want to only socialize with parents and siblings; they want to play with their peers. That's how they make sense of the world" (Boyd, 2015).

Sharing what is happening in school and conversing with teachers and peers in online communities can improve the learning experience. In a recent case study, Mandy Stewart examined the literate lives of four teenage high school students who emigrated from Mexico to the United States. She found a disconnect between "their monolingual school setting" and the "out-of-school literacies" that take place on social media, at their workplaces, and through their home country's entertainment media sources. Particularly within Facebook, these adolescents have "unique and purposeful roles . . . that allow them to connect to their home countries, maintain their Latina/o identities, acquire English, support themselves, and establish a place to succeed" (Stewart, 2014, p. 366). In another study, college students who received four text messages per week regarding course expectations, related current events, and feedback on work demonstrated higher scores on their assessments compared to students who did not receive texts in the same course (Hamm, 2015).

If applied with some thought behind it, learning communities can be formed using mobile technology and social media that is "unencumbered by the traditional structures and schedules of a classroom" (Talbert & Trumble, 2014). The students largely agree. Katie Benmar, a sophomore in Seattle, Washington, finds herself most engaged in school when teachers use the technologies that she uses in communication with friends, such as Instagram, a visual social networking service: "One math teacher has her own Instagram page where she posts homework assignments and things that she taught that day in class." Some of her teachers moved beyond posting assignments and actually provided online spaces for Katie and her classmates to share reading responses. "Participating in a discussion with other people didn't require any less thought about the book than writing a book report would have. It actually made me think about it and understand it better, because I was listening and responding to other people's opinions that were backed up with evidence, instead of following the same strict book-report format that I had been required to do for years" (Benmar, 2015, p. 23).

Technology can also help document these experiences and share them with students' families, peers, and the world. Through digital portfolios (Renwick, 2014), teachers and students document progress toward a learning goal and showcase their achievements within an online space that is accessible to families and staff. In Monica Schillinger's 2nd grade classroom,

I observed three students sitting around a table with drafts of their writing in hand. Monica asked each of them to place their writing on the table so she could scan it into their Evernote notebook. This productivity tool can take pictures of just about any artifact, house that image within an online notebook, and then share that notebook with the important people in a student's life. Taking time to acknowledge a student's hard work and using technology to communicate this accomplishment with a real audience deepens the purpose for the learning activity. This type of authentic assessment also broadens the definition of what success might look like. Monica has powerful conversations with her students as she scrolls through their digitized work while asking questions, acknowledging growth, and creating new goals. Technology used in this manner serves as a tool for engagement, not a distraction.

Example of Practice: Bring Your Own Device

Consider the following example of Melanie Kozlowski's senior English course, and how she briefly optimized the mobile technology students already had in their hands for one unit of study. Bring Your Own Device (BYOD) allows students to use their personal mobile technology for learning. For a literature study on the concept of isolation, Melanie created a nine-square menu sheet of online resources for students and sent it to her students by e-mail message using Google Docs. They could choose which book excerpts and multimedia offerings to read, listen to, and watch. Within each resource square were three ways to access the content: a Quick Response (QR) code to the online source, a hyperlinked title of the resource that the students could click on, and a short URL if the students wanted to type in the address on a desktop computer.

Melanie gave a specific date for students to discuss the content they were exploring in small groups and as a whole class. Meanwhile, these seniors were expected to take notes during their studies to answer the essential question, "How would a person seeking isolation find the experience both beneficial and risky?" Like Lisa's students in the previous section, students in Melanie's classroom worked at their own pace and provided responses in a format they chose. Students were given clear expectations about using their smartphones, tablets, or laptops within the nine square sheet: "Remember, I expect your use of digital devices to be related to our tasks and learning targets."

Then the students were off. Some of them got started right away, using their smartphones and ear buds to watch a YouTube video of an explorer showing the location in Alaska where Chris McCandless tried to survive, depicted in the nonfiction bestseller *Into the Wild* by Jon Krakauer. These students also listened to the soundtrack by Eddie Vedder from the movie about the book and read the musician's lyrics to make connections. Others accessed an excerpt of *Walden* by Henry David Thoreau to read on their mobile devices. Melanie also included recent additions to the literature canon on survival. In one of the squares, she linked an audio interview with Cheryl Strayed, author of *Wild*. As students captured their thinking within Google Docs, they shared their work with Melanie and classmates by giving them access in the settings.

Similar to Lisa's 4th graders, the seniors could now provide feedback to each other by commenting on the documents.

Melanie understands that not every student in her classroom is enamored with technology. She provides print copies of the nine square menu and of the online texts if students request them. Her practice of providing print material is consistent with recent findings that the majority of teenagers prefer reading on paper versus a screen (Rosenwald, 2015). Melanie also knows that not every student has the means to access the content she wants them to study. She gives these students the opportunity to use the desktop computers in the classroom, as well as to check out a device to use at home, the public library, or another wifi hotspot.

Melanie identified many benefits of using BYOD during her implementation of this literature unit. "First, I save having to make a lot of paper copies for students. There is also the benefit of not having to provide mobile technology for every student. They can use what they already have, be it a smartphone, tablet, or laptop. Another benefit is how this differentiated unit engages them. It even engaged the seniors who would otherwise check out at the end of the semester." She is also willing to show her students how to use the technology. For example, Melanie makes screencasts for her students to view on how to access content online or how to provide sharing rights for a document using Google Docs.

New Horizons

There's little doubt that mobile technology is here to stay. It has created a smaller world, changed how people communicate, and shaped our beliefs and values about what it means to be a citizen in our communities. The genie is not going back into the bottle. So to wall off schools from this reality with zero tolerance policies toward student use of digital devices makes us look irrelevant in the eyes of our students. When we teach our students how to use these technologies, let's remember to show them how to find balance, engage in important work and experiences, and enhance the relationships we have in front of us. I'm not suggesting a free-for-all regarding the use of mobile technology. Rather, I encourage educators to look back on what we have done and rethink how the inclusion of digital devices might serve our goals even better for deep and meaningful learning. I believe we have only started to tap into the possibilities of where these new connections might take us.

Reflection

- What about Melanie's use of technology makes it necessary?
- How might you apply her practices within your own classroom or school?

ascd | arias™

ENCORE

A CALL TO ACTION

So when is technology necessary and not just nice? Through the information, research, and examples of practice shared in this text, I hope that you have a clearer understanding about when and how educators can integrate digital tools into the classroom. This book is designed not to provide answers, but rather to pose important questions that can help you think about the problem and choose how to use digital tools in ways that can truly enhance learning.

To continue this conversation, it is up to each of us to start thinking more deeply about our own practice and that of our colleagues. For teachers, this can happen by simply reviewing a unit of study you have taught for years. Ask yourself questions such as "Are the goals for learning relevant in the lives of my students?", "How might the integration of technology at a certain point in instruction benefit the learning experience?", and "Do I enjoy teaching this unit?" If the content is not enjoyable for you to teach, your students probably won't find it fun either.

For principals and other school leaders, look for entry points where the inclusion of technology will have a clear effect on the learning experience for students. In our school, we implemented digital portfolios. This was not an initiative borne out of a need for the technology itself, but rather for the practices that would transpire because of it, such as differentiated assessment, student reflection, personal goal setting, and communication between school and home. Our journey is just one of many that any school can take. What entry points do you see in your own context?

Maybe the most important move every educator can make is to start using technology for both professional and personal learning. Start a blog and write regularly about your experiences. Create a Twitter account and connect with other thinkers and practitioners. Make a point to read and respond to the many resources available online, particularly reputable websites and reliable educators on social media. There are two main benefits. First, you become smarter and raise the collective intelligence of the learning communities you've joined. It's inevitable. Second, you will start to make connections between how you use technology and how these principles might be applied in the classroom. The possibilities are amazing.

Implementation Guide

Figure 2 includes a series of questions to promote thought and reflection as you seek to enhance instruction with technology. After each question, I've suggested tools that can be used to **access** the software and apps by students and staff alike (what technology works for us?), along with the **purpose** for practice (why use it) and potential **audience** (with whom). The list of questions is not exhaustive. I encourage you to develop your own big questions when preparing for powerful and truly connected instruction.

FIGURE 2: **Technology Benefits: Necessary or Nice?**

Are learners an active part of instruction through modeling and guided use of technology?

Examples of Access: Facebook, Twitter
Purpose for Practice: Celebrate and share learning; Model digital citizenship
Potential Audience: Family, Community, Faculty

Does the technology accommodate and differentiate for all learners' needs?

Examples of Access: Speech-to-text, Spell Better
Purpose for Practice: Provide multiple pathways to show understanding and skills
Potential Audience: Peers, Faculty

Can the technology help facilitate reflection and deepen student understanding?

Examples of Access: Evernote, FreshGrade
Purpose for Practice: Document student progress and performance; Develop relationships
Potential Audience: Family, Faculty

Are students and the classroom part of an authentic learning community?

Examples of Access: Kidblog, Edmodo
Purpose for Practice: Facilitate unique online conversations; Promote peer collaboration
Potential Audience: Peers, Faculty, Community

Can learners create content and develop new ways to present information?

Examples of Access: Book Creator, Animoto
Purpose for Practice: Publish original content; Create dynamic presentations
Potential Audience: Peers, Family, Community

Does the technology bring in an audience for learning, both near and far?

Examples of Access: Skype, Reflector, Appropriate technology-to-student ratio

Purpose for Practice: Explore distance learning; Broaden perspectives

Potential Audience: Peers, Faculty, Community

Are students provided both voice and choice with technology, thereby increasing ownership and engagement?

Examples of Access: Smartphones, Tablets, QR codes

Purpose for Practice: Increase student engagement and ownership; Add relevance

Potential Audience: Peers, Faculty, Community

Are there opportunities for students to engage in peer feedback and collaborative work?

Examples of Access: Google Apps for Education, Moodle, PoodLL, eduCanon

Purpose for Practice: Develop independence in students; Create online spaces for important work

Potential Audience: Peers, Faculty

References

American Academy of Pediatrics. (2015, October). Growing up digital: Media research symposium. Available: https://www.aap.org/en-us/Documents/digital_media_symposium_proceedings.pdf

Benmar, K. (2015, April 21). Social media: Benefit or hazard to student learning? *Education Week.* Available: http://www.edweek.org/ew/articles/2015/04/22/my-favorite-teachers-use-social-media-a.html

Boyd, D. (2015, July 15). Blame society, not screen time. *New York Times.* Available: http://www.nytimes.com/roomfordebate/2015/07/16/is-internet-addiction-a-health-threat-for-teenagers/blame-society-not-the-screen-time.html

Flipped Learning Network. (2014). The four pillars of F-L-I-P™. Available: http://www.flippedlearning.org.org/definition

French, S. (2015, March 19). Sage French asks 'What would happen if all the computers in the world suddenly disappeared?' School in the Cloud. Available: https://www.youtube.com/watch?v=LgOID552SSU

Frey, N., Fisher, D., & Gonzalez, A. (2013). *Teaching with tablets: How do I integrate tablets with effective instruction?* (ASCD Arias). Alexandria, VA: ASCD.

Hamm, S. (2015, Spring). Why texting should be part of teaching. *EdTech Magazine.* Available: http://www.edtechmagazine.com/k12/article/2015/03/why-texting-should-be-part-teaching

Hattie, J. (2009). *Visible learning: A synthesis of over 800 meta-analyses relating to achievement.* New York: Routledge.

Korat, O., Levin, I., Ben-Shabt, A., Shneor, D. & Bokovza, L. (2014). Dynamic versus static dictionary with and without printed focal words in e-book reading as facilitator for word learning. *Reading Research Quarterly, 49*(4), 371–386.

Mitra, S. (2010, July). *Sugata Mitra: The child-driven education.* TED. Available: http://www.ted.com/talks/sugata_mitra_the_child_driven_education.html.

Powers, W. (2010). *Hamlet's blackberry: Building a good life in the digital age.* New York: HarperCollins.

Renwick, M. (2014). *Digital student portfolios: A whole school approach to connected learning and continuous assessment.* Available: http://amzn.to/1E7lwDv

Richardson, W., & Mancabelli, R. (2011). *Personal learning networks: Using the power of connections to transform education.* Bloomington, IN: Solution Tree.

Robinson, K. & Aronica, L. (2015). *Creative schools: The grassroots revolution that's transforming Education.* New York: Viking.

Rosenwald, M. (2015, February 22). Why digital natives prefer reading in print. Yes, you read that right. *Washington Post.* Available: http://www.washingtonpost.com/local/why-digital-natives-prefer-reading-in-print-yes-you-read-that-right/2015/02/22/8596ca86-b871-11e4-9423-f3d0a1ec335c_story.html

Singer, N. (2014, November 16). Privacy concerns for ClassDojo and other tracking apps for schoolchildren. *New York Times.* Available: http://www.nytimes.com/2014/11/17/technology/privacy-concerns-for-classdojo-and-other-tracking-apps-for-schoolchildren.html

Stewart, M. A. (2014). Social networking, workplace, and entertainment literacies: The out-of-school literate lives of newcomer Latina/o adolescents. *Reading Research Quarterly, 49*(4), 365–369.

Talbert, T. & Trumble, J. (2014, November 27). *An education prof. goes back to high school, finds technology is no longer a tool but a context.* The Hechinger Report. Available: http://hechingerreport.org/content/education-prof-goes-back-high-school-finds-technology-longer-tool-context_18218

Toyama, K. (2015). *Why technology alone won't fix schools.* Available: http://www.theatlantic.com/education/archive/2015/06/why-technology-alone-wont-fix-schools/394727

Tucker, C. (2012). *Blended learning in grades 4–12: Leveraging the power of technology to create student-centered classrooms.* Thousand Oaks, CA: Corwin.

Related Resources

At the time of publication, the following ASCD resources were available (ASCD stock numbers appear in parentheses). For up-to-date information about ASCD resources, go to www.ascd.org.

ASCD EDge®
Exchange ideas and connect with other educators interested in Technology Benefits: Necessary or Nice? on the social networking site ASCD EDge® at http://ascdedge.ascd.org.

Print Products
Using Technology with Classroom Instruction That Works, 2nd edition by Howard Pitler, Elizabeth R. Hubbell, & Matt Kuhn (#112012)

Researching in a Digital World: How do I teach my students to conduct quality online research? (ASCD Arias) by Erik Palmer (#SF115051)

Digital Learning Strategies: How do I assign and assess 21st Century Work (ASCD Arias) by Michael Fisher (#SF114045)

The Tech-Savvy Administrator: How do I use technology to be a better school leader? (ASCD Arias) by Steven W. Anderson (#SF115015)

Getting Started with Blended Learning: How do I integrate online and face-to-face instruction? (ASCD Arias) by William Kist (#SF115073)

A Better Approach to Mobile Devices: How do we maximize resources, promote equity, and support instructional goals? (ASCD Arias) by Susan Brooks-Young (#SF116020)

ASCD PD Online® Courses
Blended Learning: An Introduction by Catlin Tucker (#PD14OC009M)

Technology in Schools: A Balanced Perspective, 2nd ed. (#PD11OC109M)

For more information: send e-mail to member@ascd.org; call 1-800-933-2723 or 703-578-9600, press 2; send a fax to 703-575-5400; or write to Information Services, ASCD, 1703 N. Beauregard St., Alexandria, VA 22311-1714 USA.

About the Author

Matt Renwick is an elementary school principal in Wisconsin Rapids, Wis. Prior to this position, he served as an assistant principal, athletic director, and elementary school teacher. Matt regularly posts on his award-winning blog Reading by Example (readingby example.com). He may be reached at mattrenwick.com or on Twitter: @ReadByExample.